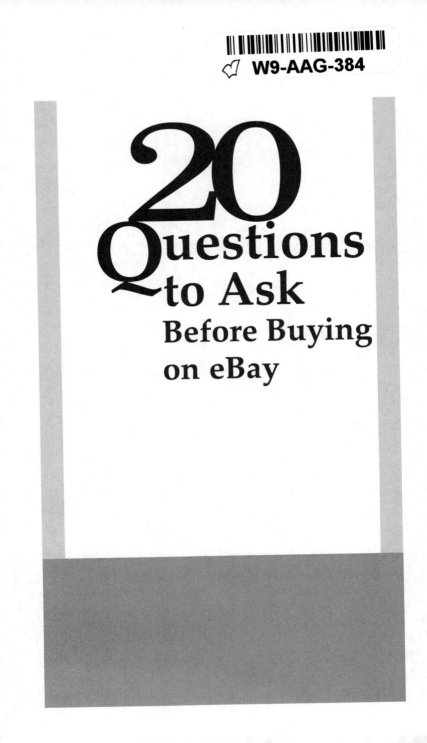

W9-AAG-384

20 Questions to Ask
Before Buying
on eBay

$1

20 Questions to Ask Before Buying on eBay

Michael Lewis

CAREER
PRESS
THE CAREER PRESS, INC.
Franklin Lakes, NJ

Copyright © 2006 by Michael Lewis

All rights reserved under the Pan-American and International Copyright Conventions. This book may not be reproduced, in whole or in part, in any form or by any means electronic or mechanical, including photocopying, recording, or by any information storage and retrieval system now known or hereafter invented, without written permission from the publisher, The Career Press.

20 QUESTIONS TO ASK BEFORE BUYING ON EBAY

EDITED BY GINA TALUCCI

Cover design by Lu Rossman/Digi Dog Design

Printed in the U.S.A. by Book-mart Press

To order this title, please call toll-free 1-800-CAREER-1 (NJ and Canada: 201-848-0310) to order using VISA or MasterCard, or for further information on books from Career Press.

CAREER PRESS

The Career Press, Inc., 3 Tice Road, PO Box 687, Franklin Lakes, NJ 07417

www.careerpress.com

Library of Congress Cataloging-in-Publication Data

Information available upon request.

Dedication

To my daughter, Sydney.
Your priceless spunk and spirit are among the few
things that can never be bought on eBay.
You'll always be my little peanut. I love you, Syddie.
(Now let me get back to finding you "My Little
Pony" stuff on eBay!)

Dedication

Acknowledgments

Thanks to my family—Amy, Samantha, and Sydney—who were forced once again to endure hours and days with me sitting and staring at the computer, tripping over books and papers. Yes, I'll take a break now and clean up a little—for at least a week or two.

Thanks also go to my literary agent extraordinaire, Marilyn Allen. If you weren't my agent, you'd still be my friend. I appreciate all your help and advice.

To the gang at Career Press: Ron Fry, Mike Pye, Laurie Kelly-Pye, Brenda Brienza, Kris Parkes, and everyone else. I miss being with you everyday but hope to see you soon.

Thanks to dear friends Lee and Janet Pfeiffer, Steve Spignesi, Barbara Murphy, Chuck Berg, and John Holliday.

Finally, thanks to fellow eBayers John Hetlyn, Phil Emaus, and my brother, Ed Lewis. Hopefully there are a few tips in here even you guys didn't know about.

Contents

Introduction

Are you the type that scours your local newspaper, searching the garage sale and flea market listings? When you know you've found a real bargain, does your heart skip a beat? Are you a busy person who loves to save time (and saving money ain't so bad either)? If you can answer yes to any (or all) of these questions, then you should consider buying on eBay.

The first time you log on, eBay can seem a little intimidating and confusing. It shouldn't be. This book is intended to give you a basic, beginner's understanding of how to buy on eBay, answering the first questions that may come to mind as you begin using the site. I'm here to give you a taste of eBay, to get you comfortable with the idea of being an eBay buyer. But I only have a limited amount of space to do so. Your job is to read the book, then log on, and jump right in. Once you're searching, bidding, and buying like a seasoned pro, then I'll recommend some other sources of information in the book's last chapter. But you need to surf around on eBay to feel comfortable doing so. With every minute you spend on eBay—surfing, searching, and buying— you'll learn something new and become more and more comfortable with how things work.

I'll happily guide you: I'm an eBay junkie. From Yankees tickets to flutes, from DVDs and baseball cards to compression shorts and movie press kits. If I can buy it on eBay, I usually do...and I usually can find bargains better than I'd find in the store. But it's easy to get addicted to eBay buying, so be careful. Don't get hypnotized by all the links and the auction excitement. And don't overpay—you heard it here first, if you can buy something cheaper and more conveniently elsewhere, then don't buy it on eBay.

I've tried to organize this book to address the questions you might be asking step-by-step in the normal course of events as you begin cruising around on eBay. Even if you've used eBay before, I suggest you read the book from cover to cover first, then go back and review some of the information that most interests you. Even if you believe you're familiar with a topic, I suggest reading through the chapter anyway—I might share a tip you haven't heard before. Both novices and seasoned eBay vets will find useful nuggets of information in *20 Questions to Ask Before Buying on eBay*. Promise!

So turn the page, fold the book open on the desk next to your computer, and let's get going. I've only got enough space to answer 20 questions (and some ancillary questions related to them). If any additional questions come up, or if you've got useful information to share with your fellow reader, drop me an e-mail at SamsPop1@aol.com. Or seek me out on eBay: my user name is SamsPop1.

Don't forget to pick up a copy of the companion guide *20 Questions to Ask Before Selling on eBay,* which holds useful information regarding the other side of the equation!

—M.L. 2006

Question 1

What Is eBay and How Does It Work?

C'mon, you mean to tell me you don't know anything about eBay?! It just happens to be the most successful, longest running, online auction on the Web, dating back to 1995. eBay is an international, online flea market, connecting folks with items to sell and those looking to buy those items. It boasts more than 135 million registered users worldwide. Millions of people sell their stuff on eBay, ranging from used garage sale-like collectible things (one man's trash literally becoming another man's treasure) to brand new, right out of the box-quality items. Millions more people just use eBay to shop and never dream of selling. Last year, $24 billion worth of goods and services changed hands through eBay; one quarter of all online purchases in the United States passing through its site.

eBay is a great place to sell things, but it caters most to people like you: buyers. You'll see—it's pretty obvious once you log on and start window shopping. There are fun things to click on everywhere, and you can search for things to buy on just about every page you happen to be looking at, just in case you think of something you want. All you have to do as a buyer is go to the site, browse around, find what you're looking for (or discover a new "something" you hadn't thought of), bid on one or more of those some-things, and hopefully win! eBay is fast, convenient, safe, and fun...even a little addicting!

> *Logging on to eBay is free and easy. You will not be asked for a name or address while you browse the site and become familiar with the layout.*

You can access eBay using a PC or a Mac and logging on to *www.eBay.com*. (I'm going to assume you have an Internet connection.) It costs you nothing to shop. Actually, let me rephrase that: You will have to pay the seller for the items you buy (plus applicable shipping, handling, and insurance charges), but eBay itself will charge you nothing for utilizing the site. However, eBay charges service fees to the sellers for the privilege of posting their auctions on the site, effectively helping them to market and advertise their wares.

So, log on and have a free look around. You won't even be asked for your name or address, at least not initially (I'll tell you when). Get familiar with the lay of the land as you surf incognito. In the next chapter, I'll go into much more detail about eBay's home page and what all those links mean.

Do I Need a High-Speed Internet Connection?

While I wouldn't say it's necessary to have a DSL, satellite, or cable modem as your high speed connection to the Internet, it sure helps move things along. I went from dial-up to DSL, and the difference in speed is like night to day (of course, if you made the same transition, you already know that). eBay is very visual, with lots of proverbial bells and whistles. If you're working with a phone connection, it takes a lot of time to load up all those flashes and photo gallery images that are included with many listings. Worst of all, you could wait and wait for an image to upload, find it won't even load at all, and then realize you've wasted valuable bidding time while you were waiting unproductively. You may decide to bid on the item sight unseen, only to be disappointed when it arrives and doesn't live up to your expectations. My advice is to invest the extra money monthly and switch to high-speed. You'll thank me for it.

By the way, eBay is an internet success story that's here to stay—a publicly held company, traded on the NASDAQ. If you enjoy your experience with the site, you might want to consider investing. It's one of the world's most profitable business models, earning millions of dollars in profits—that's a lot of 35 cent listing fees!

Question 2

What's All This Stuff on the Home Page?

Follow me. I'm more than happy to show you around the place. When you log onto *eBay.com*—although the home page may be different every time because it's constantly being redesigned—one thing's for sure: you're greeted by a blaze of colorful images and flashing icons. You can see how they are trying to make things simple for buyers with easy ways to search and find the things you're looking for, and convenient ways to browse. You can search for items several ways by typing your search request in a few different places (we'll get into more specifics about searching in the next question).

Along the top edge of the home page is eBay's navigation bar. (The navigation bar is at the top of every eBay page, enabling you to quickly get to where you need to go.) The navigation bar lets you click on *home, pay, register,* and *site map*. Just below that, you are able to click on *buy, sell, My eBay, community*, and *help*. In the upper right-hand corner there is a search box that says *start new search*. Here's what will happen when you click on those individual buttons:

- ⮯ **Home:** Clicking here always bring you back to the home page, no matter where you may be on the eBay site.

- ⮯ **Pay:** Be brought right to the list of items you've won, but have yet to pay for. PayPal is the preferred payment method of eBay.

- ⮯ **Register:** Sign up here to become a member of eBay. You don't have to do it right now, and there are other places to sign up, too. But here's one entrance to the registration area.

- ⮯ **Site Map:** Click there and have a look-see at the wealth of information available on using and understanding eBay. Read on for more details about the site map area.

- ⮯ **Buy:** This is the doorway to the *buy* area of eBay (ironically enough). You can search for items here (by typing in your search words) or browse through some of the categories mentioned. We'll get into a more detailed discussion of searching, bidding, and buying, but feel free to browse around in here. If you lose your way and forget to leave bread crumbs, remember you can always click on *home* and go back to the home page. I suggest you rummage through *buying resources* (on the right side of the *buy* page) and your comfort level should increase as you see all the info and support at your fingertips. Make a mental note of this area—everything in here might not mean much right now, but you might find yourself coming back later.

⊃ **Sell:** This is the link to seller city. We'll discuss how to sell in Question 19, but you may want to browse around and see what's available to sellers.

⊃ **My eBay**: Once you sign on to eBay, this is the page you'll use most often. Click here and proceed to your own little corner of eBay. See Question 6 for all the details and tools available through My eBay.

⊃ **Community:** This is your doorway to the eBay community and links to talk on more than 100 separate chat areas, news (press releases and news of important events), events (upcoming eBay events), people , and help (answers to most commonly asked questions and how to find live help if your answers are not readily available). Enter a keyword and find your closest match. There's a wealth of information and support to both buyers and sellers in this area.

⊃ **Help:** Another place to get answers. You can either find answers to frequently asked questions (type in words and they try to match your question with their topic), or you can get live help from a real-life person. It's comforting to know that you're protected and can get answers when you need them.

Meanwhile, back at the home page, you can see how eBay is perfect for browsing. Probably 95 percent of the things you can click on are for searching, browsing, and buying. When you're on the home page, if you see something that catches your eye, such as collectible coins, for example, click on that link and browse. Such browseable links on the home page change periodically and often reflect the seasons. Sometimes you can find real bargains on the home page. You may even see information about current charity auctions to benefit different causes. (Question 13 talks about such special auctions.)

> *Be sure to check out the very bottom of the home page where a lot of useful and often overlooked information is found. These subjects can be helpful to new users.*

At the bottom of the home page, you'll see connections to the various eBay subsidiaries worldwide, as well as other useful and often overlooked areas such as downloads (download useful information and software to make your eBay experience more meaningful), gift certificates (buy someone a gift certificate redeemable for any eBay purchase in which PayPal is accepted), Security & Resolution Center (get official help to resolve disputes), and eBay official time (when an auction is about to end, and you're in a bidding war with someone, it pays to know when the auction will expire according to the official eBay clock in California. See Questions 10 and 11 on bidding). You can browse these sections now, although they may not mean a lot to you at the outset. You will probably understand this information later, accessing from elsewhere on the site as you need help and information.

Just from this quick tour of the home page, I'm sure you'll quickly notice that there's a lot to see and do on eBay. In my opinion, it's one of the most enjoyable and most user-friendly sites on the Web. It's urging you to explore, and it's pretty easy to get help when you're confused or in trouble.

As you become more and more comfortable with using eBay, I think you'll find yourself jumping right past the home page to your My eBay page. That's where you'll do your searching and your accessing of eBay's services. (See Question 6 for more about My eBay).

Okay, go to the next question and let's start a search.

Question 3

How Do I Find What I'm Looking For?

Seek and ye shall find.

Hopefully, upon reading thus far, I've whetted your eBay appetite, you've had a bit of a look around, and now you're ready to open the doors to your cyber mall available on eBay. It's time to find something worth buying.

One of the fun aspects of using eBay is searching for items—searching is nearly as much fun as actually winning an auction. Here's how to get started with some basic searching: On the upper right area of the eBay home page, you'll see a small box. (In addition, there's a search box about one third of the way down on the home page.) Place your cursor in the box and type a few descriptive words about the particular item you're interested in. Try to be fairly specific, so you can limit your choices from among thousands of possible matches, but not so targeted that you have little to choose from. For example, if you're interested in finding a Yankees jersey and you enter just the word "Yankees," you'll probably come up with more than 50,000 matches. It's going to take you quite a while to read through all of those listings! Better to type in Yankees jersey, or Yankees shirt. See what kind of results that gets you. Theoretically, eBay may still find quite a few matches for you to look through, with your results ranging from Yankees trading cards featuring a small swatch of Derek Jeter's jersey, to gameworn Yankees jerseys (some even autographed by the player who wore them), used (let's call them "vintage") Yankees t-shirts from someone's ex-husband, and brand new Yankees pinstriped jerseys for both kids and adults (with or without Mickey Mantle's number on the back, thank you very much!). By adding more words, you narrowed your focus, but you still got back results for items that might not be right for you. To further zero in on the right matches and limit your choices even further, you might want to define your search better. We'll discuss advanced searches in Question 5.

> *eBay makes it easy to save any items that you are interested in on your My eBay page. My eBay also organizes the items you are interested in.*

So, let's say this initial search turned up a few items that looked interesting. Now what? eBay allows you to save the listings of those searched items and keep an eye on them. To do that, you need to set up your My eBay page to save and organize your searches. And to do *that*, you've now got to register. (See Question 6 for more details on My eBay).

As mentioned earlier, in your role as a buyer, using the services of eBay will cost you nothing (unless you buy an item, and then of course it will cost you to pay for it). But if you're going to search for and watch items (and eventually buy something), you will have to register (for free) so eBay knows where to store your searches.

Okay, I went off on a tangent. I'll discuss registering in a minute. Let's get back to basic searches. Besides searching for specific items, you can search for things by category. For example, let's say you're an antiques buff. You love everything to do with antiques: antiques price guides, items related to storing, restoring, and collecting antiques, and of course, the antiques themselves. On the eBay start page, you can click on the basic *antiques* category (and later, you can click on a more specific category number, once you know it), and this will bring you to the special antiques category page. You can then select from antique rugs, antique picture frames, antique polish, or whatever you are looking for.

Personally, I don't like to search this way. I think it takes too long to find the specific object I might be looking for, starting with a haystack in search of a needle. Searching by category is good for those who have time to browse, but I'm of the opinion that most sellers don't really take the time to list their item in the correct categories anyway, so why should I search that way? In other words, one seller might list a comic book in the collectibles category, another might consider it an antique and list it there, and another may put a Superman comic under the movie collectible category. If you merely searched the collectibles category, you would have missed it listed in the antiques section. In my mind, it's better to search the individual comic book you're looking for, and eBay's search engine will then find matches in any categories in which that comic appears.

And once your search results come up, eBay will suggest items in different categories that may match your search criteria as well.

When you search, it's all in the wording, that is, what words you want eBay's search engine to include, what words you want it to exclude, and so on. There are many ways you can type information into the search box, besides just entering the words. But in this chapter, I just wanted to get you comfortable with the basics of searching. (Turn to Question 5 when you're ready for some advanced searching information.) Just remember that eBay's data is entered by human beings, not some machine, and three different people could describe the same item three different ways. So I suggest you jot down different words to search that could describe the same item. Enter them into the search box and see what eBay spits out.

The following are some other search tips which you may find helpful:

➲ Search for words that appear just in the title of the auction, or in both the title and description. Obviously the latter will yield more results (maybe too many), but if you didn't tell eBay to search descriptions, too, then think of all the things you might have missed if the item name wasn't in the title.

➲ Search for Buy It Now listings. We'll get into more details about such specialty auctions, soon. But suffice it to say that Buy It Now auctions are handy when you're pressed for time and you need something right away. Such auctions offer you the opportunity to place a bid at the set price, thus winning the auction, and then you'll be on your way. When your search results come up, click the *Buy It Now* tab just above your search words, and eBay will just show you the current Buy It Now auctions that are for items similar to your search phrase.

➲ Search by item number: If you need to locate a specific item and you know the number, you can include that number in the search box and click search.

You can sort your search results any number of ways. Once you conduct a search and the results pop up, look along the left side of the page and consider the search option. You can search by proximity to you, price range, and so on. Give some of these options a try to help you sort through your search matches.

If your search yields a lot of unwelcome matches, there's a quick and easy way to winnow out the things you're not interested in, by using a hyphen. Here's how: You search for a New York Giants jersey and get quite a few responses, but you don't want women's jerseys, jerseys in kid sizes, and so on. You don't even want to look at those replica New York Giants baseball team jerseys that came up. So, on your search results page, right into the rectangular box where your search words are, type a space at the end of the phrase, then type in a hyphen (-) and list the words you don't want included in those search results. You're essentially telling eBay: I liked this search but it yielded too many items I couldn't use. So from the previous example, type in: New York Giants jersey-women's-ladies-youth-children–baseball. (You can even go the easier route and put your hyphen, followed by parentheses, include all those unwelcome terms, and close the parenthesis.) Then hit search again and you'll see all those types of auctions removed, and you'll get closer to what you need.

So, you've searched and found something (or things) you want to keep an eye on (and maybe even consider bidding on). To store these searches, you will have to register. Registering links your real identity with your eBay persona. How else is eBay supposed to know who was interested in those items? If you searched and then logged off, your search results will be lost. So now that it comes time to register, I can hear you asking:

Is eBay Safe?

When you register with eBay, you have to give your credit card number (but they won't charge you anything until you try to list and sell), as well as other personal information such as your e-mail address, street address, and so on. You can feel totally confident when you register on eBay. Your credit card will be encrypted (in layman's terms, that means the number will be encoded so no one else can abscond with it), no one but eBay will ever have your number, and nothing will be charged to you by eBay until you go and sell something. So you're safe when you deal with eBay. It's some of the sellers you have to be a little wary of, and throughout this book, I'll share with you the importance of feedback, as well as tips on how to discern the honest sellers from the shady characters (In the grand scheme of things, most eBay sellers are pretty honest, too).

Its also important to note that, while you can find just about anything on eBay, and a search in the "Everything Else" category sure turns up some "interesting" items, you will not find anything illegal for sale on eBay. And if the item is just illegal in your state, the seller couuld (and really should) refuse to sell it to you. eBay mionitors such activity and a seller shipping something illegal could be drummed out of eBay or worse.

Okay, So How Exactly Do I Register?

When you do a search and try to save the search, eBay will then prompt you to sign in. If you're new to eBay, you can click the link right on the same page, or else you can register through the eBay home page. You must be 18 to register and have an e-mail address, and you will have to acknowledge that you are willing to receive e-mail from eBay (in an effort to keep members well informed, eBay does a lot of e-mailing!). As I mentioned, you will need to have a credit card ready and answer some questions. (If you don't want to answer the demographics sort of questions, such as your household income, you don't have to. But do make sure you enter all the required information).

> *On eBay, your screen name becomes your identity. It stays with you for the rest of your eBay life, so pick something that represents you well.*

When it comes to picking a user name and password, don't pick a name that is too close of a match to your e-mail address (a mistake I made and am living with) because you could increase your chances of receiving SPAM. You don't want the wrong people to find you! Have some fun with your user name, but don't choose something potentially offensive. Your screen name is your nickname and stays with you for your entire eBay "career," so give some thought to choosing a name. Use a combination of at least six to eight letters, numbers, and characters. How about something such as Beatle01, or 1$pdrman? Choose a password that only you will know (write it down, and don't tell anyone), but if you forget your password, you'll be asked for some password hints, such as "What street did you grow up on"? By registering, you will be notified if you've been outbid on an item, whether something similar has been listed, whether an auction you seemed interested in is ending soon, and so on. These are all free services provided to buyers through My eBay. See Question 6 for more details.

What if I Want to Change My Screen Name?

I wouldn't advise it. As you'll come to realize as you keep reading (especially when you get to Question 8 and the discussion of feedback), reputation is everything on eBay. If you change your user name, it looks as though you've got something to hide, even if the change was purely innocent (you used to use the name JohnnysGal and you've since broken up with Johnny). With all the transactions you're involved in on eBay, you're trying to grow your positive reputation as someone that can be trusted, an eBayer who is a pro and pays for items won in a timely manner. If you change your name, people might ask: I wonder if she's running away from something? So my advice is to pick a user name you're comfortable with and stick with it for your entire eBay life. Some people have a separate user name for buying and for selling. Again, I'd advise against it, going back to the reputation discussion.

What if I Move or Change ISPs?

If you move, or you change your Internet service (and from that, your e-mail changes) you need to update eBay concerning your new contact info. They need to be able to find you. But such a change in locale or service shouldn't affect your eBay user name or password.

Question 4

Could You Walk Me Through a Typical Listing Page?

Now that you know a bit about searching, and you hopefully have discovered the page listing for an item that you find interesting, let me give you a little lesson on the elements of a listing, as well as the red flags to which you should pay close heed.

At the very top of the listing page, you'll see the familiar navigation bar, which should provide you with some comfort knowing it's just a click away. Just below that, you'll find information on what category this item is listed in (which is helpful if you want to search for like items, in which case you'd click on one of those categories). Below that, the majority of the page will consist of a description of the item. The seller will describe what it is he's selling, including its name, condition, age, and any other descriptive information, as well as special instructions on how this seller does business (such as shipping and payment methods). If it's a savvy seller, she'll include at least one photo of the item (or if a photo isn't there, you can ask for one. And if it's a stock photo and not an actual photo of the item you're buying, you should make it a point to ask for an actual photo). Hopefully everything is explained and described in black and white in the description. If you're not sure of something, you can ask for further explanation, and you should probably do so before you bid (see Question 9). Here's what else you'll find on a listing page. Let's start on the right third of the page:

➲ **The item number:** This can be found at the top of the right-hand column. Each item for sale on eBay, or more accurately, each eBay auction, has a different item number. Knowing this number will help you later if you need to resolve a dispute, or even if you just buy the item problem-free. It's always a good idea to remind the seller of the item number.

➲ **Watch this item:** Right under the item number, clicking here allows you to save this auction on your My eBay page. Let's not do that right now—wait until we read Question 6. But it's nice to know whenever you find something you like, all it takes is a click to save the information. (Right next to the Watch This Item link is a place to click in order to tell a friend about this auction.)

➲ **Seller Information:** This can be found next on the right hand column. You'll see the seller's user name, followed by a number in parentheses. The number represents the seller's feedback score, and following that, you'll see the percentage of positive feedback this seller has received. Following that, you'll discover how long this seller has been involved in eBay. We'll get into a full discussion on feedback in Question 8, but for now, just know this: feedback is your report card, and it stays with you. When you buy and sell on eBay, the feedback system allows each of us to rate the other's performance. How'd we do? Did this buyer pay quickly? Did this seller ship a good product expeditiously? Is everybody happy? The feedback system includes the ability to rate the transaction with that person as positive, negative, or neutral, as well as a chance to leave a brief comment. So if a seller has a high percentage of positive feedback, that means most of the comments that have been left about him were from satisfied buyers. If the number is low and the percentage of positives is low, that's cause for concern. By clicking on *read feedback comments*, the item number, or the user name, you'll be brought to that eBayer's profile page, which chronicles the feedback for this person, as well as the text of the comments she has received. See Question 8 for all the nitty gritty details. The following are some other options that you can choose when looking at a seller's item listing:

- ⮑ **Add to favorite sellers:** If this seller looks reputable and seems to be selling many things you would probably be interested in buying, you may want to save her to your My eBay page, so you can easily search her listings later. More details about this process are in the My eBay chapter.

- ⮑ **Ask seller a question:** Let's wait to discuss this until Question 9.

- ⮑ **View seller's other items:** Again, you may want to look around at what else this person is selling.

If they are set up as an eBay store, you can view their wares either through store view or list view—given the choice, I choose list view, because once you go there, you can sort further by just looking at their open "traditional" auctions, or you can choose to just look at their Buy It Now offerings. You'll understand these more as we move forward.

> *When bidding on an item, it is important to take note of all the choices on the screen. You can either choose to bid on an item or buy it immediately.*

There's not much more at the top right column you need to see. But it's good to note at the bottom of that column whether the auction (and you!) are safe under the PayPal Buyer Protection system.

Okay, now look over at the middle column on the page:

➲ **Starting bid/current bid:** This is the price the auction for this item has now reached (if no one else has bid, it's what bids start at). Just below the price is the Place Bid option. Wait! Don't touch it yet!

➲ **But It Now Price:** If that option is available for this item, this is the price you would pay if you wanted to buy the item right at that moment (see Question 12).

➲ **Time left:** This is how much time is left on the auction, in days and hours (when it's down to mere hours, they measure this in minutes and seconds). A little further down, it says the duration of the entire auction—seven days is the span most sellers choose—and just below that is the day and time the auction closes (remember, eBay time is set to Pacific time.)

⊃ **Start time:** Pretty self explanatory—the time and date the item was first put up for bid.

⊃ **History:** That's next on the hit parade. History tells you what has transpired thus far in auction including how many bids were placed, who did the bidding, and the starting bid. If you click on the bid number, you'll be shown the user IDs of the bidders, the amount they bidded, and when the bids were placed.

⊃ **High bidder:** Who is the bidder who has placed the highest bid (and next to their user name is their feedback rating. I told you that feedback follows you around!).

⊃ **Item location:** This is the location of the seller, and thus, the point from where the item will be shipped. Pay close heed to what country the seller hails from. Some people don't have a problem dealing with a seller in Europe or Asia, but there are questions and concerns that arise from a seller residing outside your country. Is the auction payable in U.S. funds? Is a DVD in China playable on a DVD player in the United States? How much, if any, additional shipping will be charged? At the risk of being politically incorrect, I've bought DVDs from China that were pirated, bootleg copies, some of which didn't even play on my DVD player. Needless to say, I won't do that again. My advice is to make every attempt to stick with new, sealed items from American sellers. There is just less chance of hassles that way. (But you know, on a positive note, you might find some rarities for sale from a seller in a foreign country. But please, just do such shopping intelligently).

⊃ **Ships to:** This tells you where the seller will ship their item. If you don't live where they ship, don't bother bidding. Actually, you could ask the seller whether he'd ship to you—maybe he just neglected to mention it. Hold that thought for Question 9, when we discuss asking the seller a question.

⊃ **Shipping costs:** The price the seller charges for shipping is mentioned here, along with what shipping method is used. At times, this might say, "see item description for details." At other times, you'll find in the listing a small box in which you type your zip code, and eBay figures out the shipping charges specific to your zip.

Further down the page, past the seller's description of her item, you'll find the following:

⊃ **Shipping, payment details, and return policy.** This goes into further delineation of the shipping costs and how the seller expects to be paid, as described previously. And as I said, this may be blank and you'll have to find such costs within the item description.

⊃ **What payment methods they accept.** PayPal is eBay's "official" payment option. Check, money order, credit cards, or some other payment methods may be accepted. To me, PayPal is the fastest and safest. (See Question 14 for more details.

⊃ **Ready to Bid?** Here's another way to place a bid, along with a recap of the item title, the current or starting bid, and a box for you to type in your maximum bid. (See Questions 10 and 11 for more information on this topic.)

Now that I've shown you the highlights of a listing page, here are a few things more red flags:

⊃ **The too-short auction:** Me being the paranoid person, I'm concerned if an auction is not seven days. Is the seller in a rush? Doing something unscrupulous?

⊃ **Stock photo:** As mentioned above, I'd like to see a real photo of what I'm buying, and not a stock photo. If you don't see one in the listing, ask to see one.

⊃ **International sellers:** Again, just be aware of where your item hails from, and that certain countries might have lower quality standards than you're used to.

⊃ **Fine print:** Read the entire listing. Ask questions. If something doesn't sound right, get the answers you need or, if you're uncomfortable with someone's terms, don't bid. For example, I'm not a big fan of going to a seller's personal payment site when an auction is over. I'll pay with PayPal, thank you very much.

What's All This COA, NWT, and MIB Nonsense?

eBay sellers love to abbreviate—I guess it's a matter of haste, like they're in a big rush. They really have as much space as they need to describe their item, so they really don't have to abbreviate. Anyway, your typical eBay listing may be dripping with abbreviations, many of which are commonly used, some of which the seller just invented. These are the ones I've seen most: BIN (Buy It Now), COA (Certificate of Authenticity), GU (gently used), GW (gently worn), MIB (mint in box), MIMB (mint in mint box), N/R (no reserve), NIB (new in box), NWT (new with tags), OP (out of print), PP (PayPal), PPD (postage paid), S/H/I (shipping, handling, insurance), VHTF (very hard to find), V/M/D (Visa, Mastercard, Discovery). But don't quote me on them, because one seller might say they mean something else. If you're not sure, ask.

Some sellers may set a reserve price on their item which is only known to them, and hidden from the buyer. They use this as protection in order to get a certain price for their item.

What's This "Reserve Not Met" Hoo-hah?

Next to an item's starting bid, you may see this notation, which is there to show you that this auction is a reserve price auction. In other words, the seller has set a reserve price for the item, which is the minimum amount she needs to receive before she can sell this item. It's an amount known only to her, and it's for her protection so she can get enough money for the item. She pays extra to list the item this way. While it provides a measure of protection to her, it can be aggravating to you the buyer, especially if you bid and bid and it still says the reserve has not been met. In other words, you can be the high bidder on an item, and if it's a reserve price auction, the seller still doesn't have to sell to you. Hopefully, if that happens, she'll wise up and lower her obviously too high reserve before she relists. More likely, she'll stick with her delusions of grandeur, her reserve price will not be met, and the auction will end with no buyer. (See Questions 10 and 11 for bidding tips.)

Hey, What Happened? Why Was This Listing Revised?

Sellers have a right to revise a listing if something has changed to the item or the auction terms, or if there was a problem with the listing. If you've placed a bid on an item, and the revision has dramatically affected the auction and your place in it, you may be able to retract your bid, if you so desire. But odds are, the revision was just to repair something minor such as a typo. If you're wondering, just ask the seller what he revised and why.

Question 5

what Is an Advanced Search?

You've searched for some items. Maybe you've even saved a few of the items you found on your watch list so you can keep an eye on them (see the following chapter for more information on My eBay). But chances are your search results turned up some items that did not quite perfectly match the things you were really looking for. Or maybe nothing was really right at all. How would you like to fine tune your search? I want to share with you some advanced search techniques and other ideas that will find you more consistent matches with what you're really searching for, now and in the future.

Let's start with some different ways of wording and punctuating your search, which could make all the difference to you:

➲ **Surround search words with quotation marks.**
If you're looking for an Indiglo watch, and no other kind of watch, type "Indiglo watch" into the search box.

⊃ **Use an asterisk when you're unsure of the spelling.** Let's say you're not sure how an item is spelled. Or maybe you're not confident that all the sellers can spell the item name properly. You're not sure if the item will be listed as Indiglo, Indigleau, Indiglou, or Indiglow. To cover yourself, type in as much as you're sure of, and put an asterisk at the very end, at the point where your knowledge ends. In other words, type "Indigl* watch." Just like that—no punctuation, spaces, and so on. The search will yield anything spelled with that base word, and any spelling variations that may follow, whether correct or not. (We'll get into typos and misspellings later in this chapter, and how you can use errors to your advantage.)

⊃ **Type in the words with a comma between them and no other spacing or punctuation.** By typing "Indiglo, watch," eBay will search for matches of either one word or the other. Such a search might result in Indiglo watches, Indiglo socks, Indiglo paint, Indiglo wigs, and so on. (I'm not sure if those things exist, but you get my drift.) It will also yield all sorts of watches—Timex, toys, pocket watches, g-shock watches, and yes...even Indiglo watches.

In structuring searches such as the previous examples, you're giving the search engine further instructions regarding your search requests.

When you did a search and you got back some results, did you notice the clickable tab called *advanced search* to the right of your search words? Click there and here's what you'll find:

⊃ **Enter keyword:** You can better define the search by adding words or rewording the search.

⊃ **Search for closed sales on the advanced search page:** You can check sale prices of similar items that have sold over the last two weeks. This is a way for you to do your due diligence, to see what other like items have sold for. Then, you can know if you'll be getting this item at a good price.

⊃ **Search by time remaining:** Whether its on the auction, price, or if the seller offers PayPal (eBay's own preferred payment system), whether the listing has at least one photo to view (a gallery listing), and more.

⊃ **In this category:** You can tell eBay what specific category you'd like it to search in.

⊃ **Search title and description; completed listings only:** We've mentioned these before. You'll yield more results by searching title and description. And you would search completed items if you're curious about what other/similar items have sold for.

⊃ **Exact phrase:** Click here and you can essentially perform a function I described previously by adding quotes or commas, that is, you can search any or all of the words, and so on.

⊃ **Exclude these words:** Tell it what not to search (serves the purpose we said before, of listing items to search with a hyphen in front).

⊃ **Items priced:** Just search for items in your price range. Why look for something that is priced way out of your ballpark?

⊃ **From sellers:** You can tell eBay to search any sellers, omit certain sellers from the search, or search only those sellers in your favorite sellers list (see the next chapter on My eBay and learn what this is all about).

⊃ **Location:** You can search the world, or just the United States. You can find items just within a certain range of your home, or you can search anywhere.

⊃ **Currency:** Choose listings that accept only certain forms of currency.

⊃ **Multiple items listing:** Search only what lots are for sale.

⊃ **Show only:** We've seen some of this earlier. That is, the ability to just search for Buy It Nows, sellers that accept PayPal, and so on.

⊃ **Sort by:** Choose if you want to view items that end first, or in order of most recent listings to oldest listings.

⊃ **View results:** You can look only at auctions that include picture galleries with the listing.

There are many ways to find an item that you are interested in. eBay makes it easy to sort through all of the listings by making it conenient to your needs.

Okay, back up to the search results page for more search criteria, which appears on the left side of the page.

You can search here for related items in that category, or access some of the other search options here that we spoke about earlier. Again, eBay is constantly trying to make things easily accessible for buyers; that's why you might see similar things in several different places.

As I explained earlier, be aware that different people define things differently. Think of synonyms, or different words to describe the items. And also be aware that people make typing mistakes. Intentionally misspell words in the search box. eBay will not give you a spelling grade, but it will find any auctions featuring those misspelled words. While most people are searching for the item by spelling it right, there will be few bids for the items that are spelled wrong. You may be able to snatch it right up with little competition. Their loss is your gain. Just think of ways someone might misspell something and look around.

What if, After All This Searching, I Still Don't Find Anything That's Just Right?

Okay, Goldilocks, for people such as you, eBay has Want it Now, a chance for you to send out an All Points Bulletin of what you're looking for, in the hopes that some eBay seller has got one. You can get to the Want it Now option via the eBay home page (among other places). Click on *Want it Now* on the buyer's side (the left), and you'll come to a page on which you will type the item title and description. The post gets placed on eBay and if a seller has got something you're looking for, he'll post an auction...and hopefully you'll bid on and buy the item. Of course, there are no guarantees on either side. Buyers cannot be guaranteed that someone will post an item for them, and sellers can't be so sure that someone will, in fact, buy the item, even if they purposely list it for someone. But in a perfect world, let's hope that the buyer and seller hook up and we all live happily ever after.

Q*uestion* 6

What Is "My eBay"?

My eBay is your eBay—your own little private corner of the eBay Website. It's the place where you do business, whether you're buying, selling, or both. Via My eBay, you can view the items you're watching, bidding on, what you've won, organize your search, favorites and preferences, sort and compare, and more.

To get your own My eBay page, as a buyer, you'll need to register with eBay. As I mentioned earlier, it's free to do so and completely safe. Once you register, you'll go to My eBay again and again, as soon as you sign on to the site, because that's the place where you can view your eBay activities, as well as the status of your bids and winnings. (If you haven't already done so, read Question 3 for details on registering.

Once you've set up your My eBay page, you should click on that link as soon as you type in the eBay.com URL address. At that point, you'll be asked to sign on to eBay with your user name and password, and you will then be brought directly to My eBay.

Here's what you'll see on the My eBay page, and how to use all the page's tools to your best advantage. (I'm going to describe the default layout of the page; you can always organize your page differently by clicking on the "customize" buttons throughout the page, or changing your preferences.) Let's start by looking through the stuff on the right-hand two thirds of the page, the biggest section of the page.

- ⮑ **Welcome:** At the top, you'll notice you're being welcomed to the page with your screen name. If for some reason that's not you (such as you're looking at your friend's My eBay page), then you may want to log them out and log yourself in.

- ⮑ **My Messages:** This is just below your warm welcome. It's where eBay will post important messages about eBay in general, or some nugget of information you alone need to know (such as an update on an auction dispute).

- ⮑ **Buying Reminders:** This is where eBay tells you if/when someone might have outbid you on an auction that's still running. Hurry over and up your bid if you want it!

- ⮑ **General eBay Announcements:** More news from the mother ship.

- ⮑ **Items I'm Watching:** You can store up to 100 auctions in order to observe their progress. They can be further separated as "all," "active," and "ended" (yes, eBay stores ended auctions here, too, so you may have to delete them at times to save space). You can sort your watch list any number of ways: by price, auction ending date, seller ID, and so on. This allows you to price compare and decide if/when you want to place a bid on something.

⊃ **Items I'm Bidding On:** Next on the hit parade. Pretty self-explanatory. If you've bid on an item, it will be shown here. If you are a bidder, but no longer the high bidder, you can place a bid right off of its listing on My eBay. And bear in mind that when you bid on something that was in your watch list, it will still be shown in your watch list unless you go in and delete it.

> *"My eBay" is your eBay and you can customize it any way you'd like to enhance your eBay experience. All of your information will be stored in one, easy to access place.*

⊃ **Items I've Sold:** Last but not least of the watch sections. Obviously, if you haven't sold anything yet, then nothing would be listed here.

Okay class, now turn your attention to the extreme left side of the page, where you find My eBay views and related links. My eBay views allows you to look at different things you're watching. In other words:

⊃ **My Summary:** That's the view we were first looking at. If you decide you don't need a summary of everything, then you can click on one of the other views. But if you want to go back to a summary, click here.

⊃ **All Buying:** This affords a closer look at what you're bidding on and buying. Click on *watching* and you will go just to the items you're watching. Click on *bidding* and you can see what you're bidding on at a glance. Following that is the "best offers" option, where you can offer sellers your best offer on selected auctions. It's up to them whether they accept or deny it. "Won and didn't win" options are next after that. Finally, under "all buying" is "personalized picks," a new service in which eBay finds items it believes match some of the types of items you seem to be watching and buying.

➲ **All Selling:** Each of these tabs affords a closer look at your selling activity—scheduled, selling, sold, and unsold.

➲ **My Messages:** Goes solely to those messages that eBay has posted for you. Once there, you can also contact a member and eBay, if needed.

➲ **All Favorites:** This is a nice convenience. You can use your My eBay page to store your favorite searches, your favorites sellers, or your favorite categories. These services will save you lots of time. For example, if you're constantly looking for Tiffany lamps, the next time you search for them, click *save search* on the search results page and the search is saved. Then you can go in later to favorite searches and just click on that search and it will be conducted. If there are sellers you see yourself buying from continuously, store them here, and you can just search their wares (and no one else's) later. (Note that you can only store a finite number of favorites.)

➲ **My Account:** View the information personal to you and your account. Go into the preferences section to customize how you want eBay to display things, and how you want them to e-mail you with updates on auctions that are to expire soon, when you've won an item, and so on. (You can access feedback here, but I tend to post feedback through "Items I've Won," rather than here. Its easier to keep track that way.)

Further down that column are links to other locations on eBay that we'll talk about later in the book (you probably won't access them through My eBay but they're here if you need them).

Now that you're a little more familiar with My eBay, have fun saving auctions on it, and then sorting through those auctions.

Question 7

How Do I Know I'm Getting Something at a Good Price?

Before you make any important decision in life, you should always do your due diligence. Check things out to make sure you're getting a good deal. That goes for buying on eBay, too. You might think I'm making too much of this, but I'm someone who doesn't want to feel like I've been taken advantage of. Before you ultimately spend your hard earned money, you should feel you're getting the item you desire at a competitive price that you're happy with. If what you're looking to buy is something you've been thinking about for a while, odds are you know what the approximate cost should be, and what you're willing and able to pay. Hopefully you can find what you want at the right price on eBay.

To illustrate, let's say you are in the market for a pair of those trendy Under Armour compression shorts. You've seen them worn by your favorite basketball players, and you can see yourself wearing them while you work out at the gym. They were on sale for the same price in the sales flyers of two competing local sporting goods stores. You then were at Wal-Mart and noticed another brand for a little bit less. You might be well-served looking on Amazon for the item (they tend to have everything on that site), and also doing a Google search of the item, to see who else online might be selling that item. Make a mental note of the prices (be sure to consider adding appropriate sales tax, and shipping if applicable).

Now, log on to eBay and have a look-see. Conduct a search on eBay for the item. Hopefully you'll find a plentiful supply of open auctions. If not, the product may be rare, or in high demand and low supply, at least as far as eBay is concerned. In such cases, eBay sellers will be able to get more money for the item, so you may wind up buying it locally because no bargains will be found on eBay. (Remember to always add in shipping, handling, tax, and any other charges the seller might be charging, in doing your price comparisons).

Before you put in a final bid for an item, it's important to shop around other locations first. The item may be available somewhere else for a cheaper price.

But let's just say you've found a fair amount of compression shorts in your size from which to bid. Store them on your watch list. Now, do the same search, but look for completed transactions. When the search results come up, look along the left-hand side of the page and scroll down to the "show only" area and click on *completed listings*. Then, just below that, click on the *show items* bar. You will then be shown all auction sales of similar items that have closed within the last two weeks. Then you can see what others have recently paid for the items you're thinking of.

If you're unsure of which type of item to buy, which manufacturer or model is the best, and so on, then go to the eBay home page and click on *reviews and guides.* eBay provides you with ratings, reviews, and shopping guides. For example, if you're considering buying a new camera, you can search the digital camera guide and get background information about the different types of cameras, accessories you'll need, consumer ratings, and more. You may also refer to such trusted sources as Consumer Reports for product information and reviews. Or stop by your local electronics store and get some guidance.

So here's the happy recap: search online, on eBay, and in your local stores to see what the items you are considering have sold for. Check out the prices paid in recent auctions as well. Once you are sure the price is right, then place a bid. (See Question 10 for more details on bidding.)

In the next chapter, we'll talk about how to do your due diligence of sellers, using the eBay feedback system.

Question 8

What Is Feedback and Why Is It Important?

Feedback is a mirror reflecting on you, a spotlight on how you do business, and the first impression you are giving to the eBay community, following you around wherever you go on the site. You are your feedback. Are you an honest and reputable person? Just as importantly, is the seller of the item you're considering a "positive" seller? Read through some of her feedback and find out. Often, an eBay seller may not sell to someone who has had very little feedback posted, or who has received too much negative feedback, so it behooves you to start off right with positive feedback.

Feedback is how buyers and sellers judge each other's honesty, integrity, and the way people are conducting business—everyone's public record, if you will. So if you want to do business on eBay, it behooves you to do business honestly, thus illiciting positive feedback from people with whom you have done business. As a buyer, it behooves you to be aware of the track record of a prospective seller. Has she been an eBay seller for a considerable amount of time? Has she handled many transactions? Does she have a high percentage of positive feedback?

> *As a first time buyer, it is always important to make a good first impression. If you are unsure of something, ask the seller before getting in over your head.*

Note: If you're just starting out on eBay, you're sometimes looked at almost derisively by sellers. They are a little wary, dealing with eBay novices. As mentioned, some people may not even agree to do business with you, or at the very least, they may want you to ask permission before you bid (read the fine print on the listing). So, for your first few transactions, go out of your way to do everything right: communicate with the seller once the transaction closes ("I'm the winning bidder of this auction, here's my address, I look forward to receiving the item"), pay promptly (most sellers expect payment within three days and if not received, the seller will relist the item and post negative feedback against you), don't bid unless you intend to pay, and be pleasant in every way. Do what it takes to build up a cache of positive feedback so it will be easier for you to do more business with others in the future.

Let's back up a little: Every time an eBay transaction closes, both buyer and seller have the ability to rate each other through the feedback system. You cannot leave feedback unless you're someone involved in the transaction, that is, either the winning buyer or seller. While it is not mandatory to leave feedback, it's just a good way of doing business. It gives future buyers and sellers a thumbnail report on the transaction that just took place, and provides some insight regarding the business practices of the buyer and seller. When a transaction closes, you have a choice of leaving positive, negative, or neutral feedback. eBay provides several places where you can click to leave feedback, and often reminds you to do so.

Besides clicking one of those three choices, you can leave a text message of up to 80 characters. I find this almost not enough space and, like me, you'll have to learn to say only the highlights, with abbreviations and no punctuation. A humble request: if you're going to leave a text message, can you make it meaningful? If you're literally going to write blah, blah, blah, why not forego leaving a message? You're not really helping anyone. If on the other hand, you can shed some light on the seller and the transaction that just took place, such as, "Great communication and quick delivery. Recommended seller," then do so. We future buyers will be much obliged for your insight and guidance!

In my opinion, as a buyer, you shouldn't leave feedback for the seller immediately after an auction closes. Instead, wait until you have received and inspected the item (but less than 90 days from the closing of the sale). (See Question 15 for more information on receiving your order.) If you have any problems whatsoever, take it up with the seller before you leave your negative feedback. Disputes can often be resolved before feedback is left, because it's often very difficult to remove negative feedback once it's been left. I always like to give sellers the benefit of the doubt and give them every chance to right a wrong. But if for some reason the seller is just not cooperating, then by all means, leave negative feedback.

> *After you've bought an item from a seller, it is better to wait until you receive your package and inspect it before leaving any type of feedback.*

But bear in mind that if you are the first to leave feedback, the seller can respond and blast you back with negative feedback. Even if you've left positive feedback for a seller, he can turn around and leave negative feedback for you anyway. While you might have thought everything went smoothly, maybe he had an axe to grind. Maybe he wasn't impressed by the way you did business, or maybe he's just a jerk. So you may just want to hold off just a little while on leaving your feedback, at least until you've received positive feedback and/or you're confident that you will receive positive feedback in the near future. At times, feedback is your only recourse after a transaction closes, so you may want to hold it in abeyance. Finally, if someone leaves negative feedback for you, after you left feedback, you can respond to his negative feedback and provide further comment, almost like a rebuttal. But do your best to avoid that "he said, she said" act. Be a good buyer on eBay and you can avoid that nonsense. And remember what mom said: If you can't say something nice about someone, don't say anything at all. Loosely translated for eBay: If you're mildly unhappy with a seller, better to not leave negative feedback, or he could return the "favor," tenfold. I tend to leave negative feedback when I'm left with no other choice: the eBay community must be warned about this yutz. Because remember, both negative and neutral feedback lowers your overall feedback number.

Can Anyone Leave Feedback for Anyone Else?

Only the two people—a buyer and seller—directly involved in a closed transaction listed on eBay can leave feedback for each other. If that weren't the case, then you could go around and leave feedback for anyone who might have outbid you at the last second on an item. Not fair.

What if I Feel I Received Negative Feedback Unfairly?

If you're unhappy with the feedback a seller has left for you, first try taking it up with the seller and plead your case. Then, contact eBay thru buyer services and tell them (via e-mail) what happened. They are usually pretty good at handling disputes and will only remove negative feedback if both sides agree to it, because it was unwarranted.

How Can I Better the Odds of Receiving Positive Feedback?

As mentioned, do your best to be a good buyer. Communicate rapidly, politely, and effectively with the seller. Pay promptly. Be pleasant and hassle-free. Question item descriptions, terms, and fees before the auction closes, not after. Make the transaction as smooth as possible for the seller, with minimal headaches. And don't deal with sellers that are jerks—you can check the feedback that has been left for them and that they have left for others. If they seem as though they have a chip on their shoulder, beware. You may want to buy from someone else. Make sure you read comments left about the seller and you don't just consider their feedback rating and percentage.

I Bought More Than One Item From a Seller. Do I Have to Leave Feedback for All the Transactions?

You don't have to leave feedback for anyone, but you *should* leave feedback for every transaction, although only one of them gets counted towards the seller's feedback tally. But your description of the auction can be different for each sale, and, as mentioned, you're providing important insight into the transaction and the seller's selling practices.

Should I Do Business With a Seller "Boasting" Low, or Very Little, Feedback?

Who are you, Mother Theresa? All kidding aside, I guess it depends on how magnanimous you feel. If the seller has low feedback simply because they're just starting out on eBay, then they may be worth taking a chance on. When you're just starting out, wouldn't you like someone to come and play with you? If she seems like she's honest and trustworthy, offers guarantees, lets you pay by PayPal, and the feedback she's gotten so far has been positive, give her a try. If, however, the seller has little feedback because most of the feedback she's received is negative, especially if the negative feedback is recent, then I think you should steer clear of that seller. Maybe ask them a question to gauge their responsiveness and helpfulness. Read the comments buyers have posted and see—maybe the person was having problems at home, sometimes there's just no pleasing a buyer, and some may have just wanted to get on their soapbox and blast someone with negative feedback. If this low-rated seller is the only one selling what you want, you may have no other choice but to deal with her. Note that feedback of 90 percent means 1 of 10 was a negative. However, the seller's negatives might have been in the past and well behind them. Look closer. (And by the way, sometimes extremely high feedback numbers aren't so great, either. They may indicate that this seller is doing so much business on eBay, how do you know you won't get overlooked and wait too long for the service you deserve?)

> *There may be a lot of different reasons why a seller doesn't have good feedback. Be sure to read what other buyer's wrote before ruling out a certain seller.*

How Can I Build My Own Positive Feedback Fast?

There are several ways: Participate in Buy It Now auctions or buy something that is ending soon. Pay quickly. Communicate. Leave positive feedback for the seller and ask them to leave a positive for you—some need a nudge.

What Do Those Little Sunglasses Mean Next to Someone's User Name?

When an eBayer changes their eBay identity, the site will show sunglasses next to their new user name. If the change was necessitated by their running away from negative feedback, or because they're trying to hide out for another reason, that's a concern. What are they afraid of us knowing? If you're going to choose to do business with such a person, you may want to ask him what happened, and why his identity changed. If you don't get an answer that shows the person to be honest and reputable, maybe you should work with someone else. But if the person is new to eBay, those sunglasses will stay there for 30 days, just to alert people to the fact that you're a little wet behind the ears. If you're unsure about the reason for a person's sunglasses, it's good to question why.

And What Do Those Stars Next to Someone's Feedback Mean?

After your 30 days, the sunglasses will disappear, and eBay's star system takes effect. Colored stars are badges of honor on eBay, ranging from yellow (10-49 positive feedback) to a red shooting star (more than 100,000 happy customers). They show that you've been in the trenches, nurturing your positive feedback. If you want to know what the individual colors mean, run your mouse over the number.

My final bit of advice concerning the important subject of feedback: Start off not trusting anyone on eBay, then lower your guard from there. Feedback is a barometer of an eBayer's honesty, integrity, and customer service. Without such a rating, how else could you ever do business with strangers?

Question 9

How Do I Ask the Seller a Question?

Questions often arise while an auction is open, and even after it closes. If you're thinking of bidding, better to make sure that you understand all the terms and conditions before you bid, not after.

You communicate with a seller by e-mailing her through eBay. When you're on the auction listing in question, click on *ask seller a question* on the right-hand side. This brings you to a page on which you are to type your question right into a box, with no more than 1,000 characters. Underneath, you will be asked whether you want to hide your e-mail from this seller (that's up to you), or whether you want a copy of this question sent to your own e-mail (I recommend you do, so you can determine how long it takes the seller to respond). Please note that the seller may include your question and his response in an update to the auction listing. Because it's posted right on the site, it's helpful to the seller to answer it once, then post the answer for all the world to see. You might benefit someone else with the same question, and this saves the seller some time and effort of having to e-mail multiple potential buyers all asking the same question. So, if you post a question, watch the site (as well as your e-mail) and wait for your response.

So what kind of questions could you ask? Anything really, it's up to the seller whether she wants to answer (although it would be silly for her not to). Some questions could include variations of:

- ➲ Can you better describe the item, giving more details on its condition?
- ➲ Can I see a photo of the item (maybe a different angle, or at a higher resolution)?
- ➲ What are your ship costs (if not adequately described in the listing)?
- ➲ Is the item new, used, clean, factory sealed?
- ➲ What ship method do you use? Can I get the shipment insured?
- ➲ Do you offer a guarantee?
- ➲ Is there a discount on shipping if I win multiple items from you?

When bidding on an item, always make sure you read the entire ad. If you are unsure of something, don't hesitate to e-mail the seller and ask them a question.

Basically, if there's something that's not clear, or something you're concerned about, don't be afraid to ask. The only dumb questions are the ones you don't ask. A good seller has nothing to hide.

I E-mailed the Seller a Question and Heard Nothing Back. Now What?

If you ask a seller a question and you get no response, or it takes seemingly forever for the seller to respond, consider yourself forewarned. Actions speak louder than words, and by not responding to you soon—or not at all—the seller is giving you a little insight into their reputation and the way they do business. You asked them a specific question about their item and they didn't respond. Do they have something to hide? Or maybe they answered you, a week after their auction expired (with no bids, by the way), and they had a surly attitude suggesting you were bothering them. What does this say about their customer service and attention to detail? Are they too busy to help a potential buyer? How quick will they be to ship you your winnings? Okay, you can say I'm being paranoid, or maybe that poor seller is going through a health challenge, has been away on business, or there's something else distracting him from eBay. But everyone deserves to be treated with professionalism and respect. And you know what? There are thousands of other sellers out there, who are more than willing to work with you. So if you're not getting a good vibe from someone, move on.

Question 10

How Do I Place a Bid?

Now that you've found something you like, you're familiar with the terms of the listing, and you haven't already been priced out of the ballpark, then put your money where your mouth is. It's time to state your intentions. It's time to place a bid.

Placing a bid is easy, winning is quite another. Remember that a bid is a contract, and it is not to be rendered lightly. By bidding, you're entering into a business deal with that seller. Much like a marriage, you have to go into this with your eyes wide open and with clear intentions. A bid is a promise from buyer to seller that, if you win, you intend to pay, so don't bid over your head, or for something you really don't want (although under rare, certain circumstances you can retract a bid. More on that later).

Now that you understand the seriousness of bidding, here's how to place a bid: While you're looking at the item listing page, you can click right near the top, where it says *place bid*, or you can go further down the page, below the item description, and type your bid amount right in that box. Make sure you enter the correct amount, and that the decimal point is in the right place. Please note that you can't bid below the opening bid amount, or less than the current bid amount (that might be obvious to most, but I just thought I'd say it for everyone else's benefit).

So after you place your bid, eBay will ask you to confirm the amount, and then you will be told the status of your bid. Are you the current high bidder? Have you been outbid? How much time is left? Once you place a bid, the auction goes into your "Items I'm Bidding On" section of your My eBay page. (It will also stay in your "Item's I'm Watching" section, unless you delete it there.)

> *There are a couple of options when it comes to bidding. eBay has a program that will bid for you (up to a certain amount specified by you).*

When you place a bid, eBay is asking you for your maximum bid amount. You can bid just above the next bid increment, or you can, in fact, tell eBay the maximum amount you're willing to bid. eBay will then do the bidding for you, which is called proxy bidding. For example, you decide to bid on a collectible *Life* magazine with the Beatles on the cover. There's a current bid for $1, and the next minimum bid needs to be $1.25. You can choose to bid just $1.25 (and provided no one else bid a higher amount earlier, you would then be the high bidder), or you can type in your maximum bid amount. You decide this magazine is worth $5, so that's your maximum bid amount, and that's what you enter. eBay posts your $1.25 bid, and holds in abeyance the rest of what you're willing to bid. If someone else comes along and bids $1.50 as their maximum bid amount, their bid will be registered, but eBay will quickly enter your bid of $1.75 and you're still the current high bidder. And so it goes, until the auction ends. And not to worry, eBay will never place a bid for you that exceeds what you told it to bid.

Proxy bidding is convenient, but you should still monitor it. Someone can obviously bid past your maximum amount. If you're not alert, and you don't up your bid, they can win the item, often for little more than your maximum bid. (When you are ready to get into some advanced eBaying, you can buy software that will automatically bid for you. Until then, just keep an eye on things.) And note that with proxy bidding, it pays to place bids early, because in the case of a tie, the earliest bidder wins.

If I'm the Current High Bidder, Can I Up My Bid?

By all means, you can increase your maximum bid, as protection against outbidders. Just go to the item listing page, click on *place bid*, and enter your new maximum bid amount. eBay may never have to place a proxy bid for you, but at least your funds will be there if necessary.

I just told you a little about simple bidding. Now let's get into some advanced bidding tips and tricks:

➲   **Bid in odd increments:** If there's a current bid for the item, let's say for $2.25, and the next bid increment will bring the bidding price to $2.50, bid an odd amount, such as $2.52, or $2.78. You're trying to think a few steps ahead of your competition, which is especially useful when the auction is about to end and the bidding gets fast and furious. Bid a few pennies beyond what the competition could be bidding, and a few steps past the minimum bid. You only have to win an auction by one cent to be the winner.

⮞ **Place bids during the wee hours:** The fact is most eBay customers are located on the east coast, so most of them will be bidding around the same time. Why not outbid them during off season/ nonpeak times. When they're snoozing, you'll be running off with some great auction winnings.

⮞ **See what else the seller is selling:** Maybe Mr. Seller has other things you might be interested in. He can combine shipping on your winnings, as the seller can pack everything into one box. And if the seller has several auctions for the same item, you might decide it's better to bid on one, rather than continue in a bidding war for another.

⮞ **Shadow your competition:** If you keep seeing the same user ID names following you around, chances are this person is interested in the same type of items you're interested in. It might be a good idea to do some research on this person— check his feedback, click on the individual auctions he's won, then search to see what else that buyer might be selling. You can also search by bidder when doing an advanced search. Again, when you see what your rival is bidding on, you can then keep an eye on him, see what sellers he frequents, where he's located, and when he bids (so you can see about swooping in and outbidding when he least expects it). Ostensibly, you're letting someone else do your homework and finding some things for themselves that you're interested in, too. Another way to spy on your competition and maybe pre-outbid them is to go to an open auction page for an item you're interested in and click on bid history. This will show you who's bidding on what, and when. You can then see what else this bidder might be bidding on and place a bid yourself.

⊃ **Be a sniper:** I alluded to this previously. Sniping is the practice of waiting until the last seconds of an auction in order to outbid rivals and win the auction. You do this by keeping the auction in your watch bin, and monitoring when the auction will close. (You may want to be doubly prepared by synchronizing with eBay's clock, so you can be completely sure when an auction will end.) Of course, in order to snipe, you have to be ready to quickly bid—and outbid—right as an auction is about to end. If the auction is to end at 2:43 a.m....well, that's up to you if you want to snipe at that time. If you're a serious sniper, you may want to utilize some of the software that is available online that does the sniping for you. But for now, give sniping a try yourself. It's fun and exciting, and a bit of a battle. You may get discouraged and lose to a rival sniper, or you may be the winner. Luck and timing have a lot to do with your success.

Can I Retract My Bid?

As I mentioned, a bid is a binding contract and it can only be retracted with the help and consent of eBay. There are only a few cases where you can do so. For example, if the amount of your bid was obviously entered wrong (such as you moved the decimal point one place to the right), the seller revised his listing and the item's new description has changed dramatically from the version you bid upon, or you're not able to locate the seller on eBay. I suppose you could retract a bid if the seller agreed to let you do so, but I wouldn't count on that happening.

Question 11

What if I'm Outbid?

Well, that all depends on when you were outbid. If the auction is still active, you can decide whether you still want to participate in that auction and bid again. If being outbid enabled someone else to win the auction, the party's over and you're going to have dive back in, searching and bidding again.

If you were one of the bidders in the running for an item, and the auction is still open and active, then it's up to you whether you're willing to pay more for the item. Have you reached your spending limit? How badly do you want this item? If you bid more, will it still be a good price? Can you get the item somewhere else for a cheaper price? And as I trust you know, just because you decide to up your bid, it doesn't mean you're guaranteed to get the item. You may be outbid again. Sometimes you just have to know when to say when.

Before you consider bidding again, let me suggest that you look around eBay further. Is someone else selling the same item for less? Might this same seller have that very same item available, maybe even at a lower price? Search through that seller's other items, as sellers often put up for bid several of the same items simultaneously.

Let's say you've searched eBay and there's nothing else like the item you were hankering for. That's good news for the seller and not such good news for you. That's called supply and demand, and if there's a scarcity of product and a surplus of buyers, then the price can be driven up as more people scramble to bid on it. Be careful you don't get pulled up into the vortex of a bidding war and wind up paying more than you can afford. Confucius say: Better to lose than overpay. But if you want to continue battle bidding, check the last chapter again for some advanced bidding techniques.

Before bidding on a certain item, take a look around eBay and see if anyone, even the same seller, is selling the exact item for a lower price.

Were you outbid the instant after your bid was placed? That happens quite often. If someone else had bid on the item, and they are the current highest bidder, and you come along and outbid them, they can instantly outbid you. Technically, it was eBay itself that outbid you. That earlier bidder had placed a bid and then told eBay the maximum amount they would bid. And as we mentioned earlier about proxy bidding, eBay will automatically bid for the bidder, up to their maximum bid amount. So if you then come along and bid less than that original bidder's maximum bid amount, then you will instantly get outbid. But, if you outbid that person's maximum bid, then you will now be the highest bidder. Have I confused you yet? As you get in the trenches and do it, I think you'll see what I mean.

Was I Sniped?

If, by chance you were outbid by someone seemingly at the last second, just before the auction was to expire, then you were the victim of a "drive-by sniping," the advanced bidding tactic we discussed in the last chapter. Master the art of sniping and maybe you, too, can swoop in and scoop up a bargain at the last minute. It's kinda fun—unless it keeps happening to you. So you might want to consider your karma and limit how often you snipe someone.

I Thought I Lost – What's This Second Chance Offer?

At times, a seller can offer bidders a second chance offer. In other words, you might be able to buy the item at the last amount you bid. And why would a seller do this? Maybe she's got more than one of the item and is willing to let a second (or third or fourth) go at a little bit less (that is, your losing bid) rather than relist the item. Second chance offers are offered at the seller's discretion—she doesn't have to extend an offer, and if your bid wasn't high enough she might not. If you get an e-mail from the seller with a second chance offer—and provided you haven't bought the same thing from another auction—then consider yourself lucky. Go for it.

Question 12

What Is "Buy It Now" and How Does It Work?

Buy It Now is a great way to get an item right away. Here's how it works: A seller lists an item for sale and includes a Buy It Now price. That's the price he's willing to take right at this moment. He'll part with his item for that much, and its yours if you think the price is right.

Sometimes a Buy It Now price is the only price offered in a particular auction, and when you place a bid the auction is completed and you've won. And sometimes, the current bid price and a more expensive Buy It Now price are listed simultaneously. You might just decide to bid the current bid, but still not pay the Buy It Now price. That's up to you, but you run the risk of being outbid—either by someone upping your current bid, or by another bidder who decides they want to buy it now.

The attraction of utilizing Buy It Now is that you'll get the item sooner, rather than later. You don't have to wait for the auction to run its full duration, or run the risk that you'll place a bid, wait, and then get outbid and lose. Let's say it's an auction for tickets to a football game and you want the tickets right away because the game's coming up soon. The Buy It Now price seems pretty decent to you, and you don't mind paying a little more to Buy It Now so you don't have to wait. In that case, click *Buy It Now*. (And by the way: If you bid on Buy It Now, it's expected that you'll pay immediately, if not sooner.) Another plus is that sometimes the seller will pick up the shipping charges on their Buy It Now auction.

Buy It Now is a fast way to get an item you really want. Instead of waiting to win an auction, you can buy the item for a price set by the dealer. Most of the time, this price will be listed right next to the current bid price on the items page.

One little tip: When you see something you like as a Buy It Now, save the listing on your watch page. Then, have a look through the other items that seller might be offering. You might find the same item much lower priced in a "traditional" auction. If it's ending soon, and you don't need it right away, it just may be worth it to bid on the "regular" auction instead of the same item. Sellers often list items several different ways.

But if you've saved a Buy It Now auction on your watch list, just beware that someone can swoop in and "Buy It Now," right under your nose.

Please note, as we mentioned earlier, when you search for an item, and you get your search results, you can then just search among those results for any auctions that might be Buy It Now items. Just click the *Buy It Now* tab.

So for expediency, usually at a decent price, use the Buy it Now technique.

Question 13

What's a Dutch Auction?

Tulips! Get your Tulips! Who will me give $1 for this bulb?! No, it's not that kind of an auction.

A Dutch Auction allows a seller to put up for sale in one auction multiple identical items. Such auctions are especially helpful for the seller who finds himself with several of the same item. It saves him from having to relist the same items repeatedly. The only downside to the seller is that he agrees to sell all of his items at the same winning price. If that price is relatively low, good for you, but bad for Mr. Seller. As a buyer, you can bid on one or more items—just enter the quantity you want right in the box (the auction will tell you how many total items are for sale).

Dutch Auctions are becoming more and more of a rarity on eBay, and I'm not sure why. Perhaps sellers have decided they don't want to limit the prices of their items, and will take their chances (and the extra time and listing fees) selling each item individually.

20 Questions to Ask Before Buying on eBay

Besides "traditional" eBay auctions and Dutch auctions, there are several other types of auctions that sellers can utilize, with pros and cons for both buyers and sellers:

➲ **Live auctions.** While these affairs may be exciting—think Sothebys Auction House on the Web—you may want to forego them, at least early on in your eBay buying career. Live auctions can be high pressure and high priced. While you may find rare items here, there is not much of an item description in live auctions, a dearth of photos, and a buyer premium attached to each sale. It might be a case of "a nice place to visit, but I wouldn't want to buy here."

➲ **Charity auctions.** Sometimes eBay gets involved in auctioning things for charity. For example, they might auction off props from the most recent season of *Survivor* in order to assist hurricane victims. These auctions seem pretty steep at times, but after all, they are for good causes.

➲ **Reserve price auctions.** We touched on this a little back in Question 2. In these auctions, a minimum reserve price is placed on the item by a seller, representing the least amount of money she'd accept for that item, an amount known only to the seller. While I can understand the reason for doing this—so the seller doesn't get burned by someone paying less than what the seller even paid—I think reserve auctions can often frustrate the buyers. I've bid on such auctions and find myself increasing my maximum bid amount to the point where I just grumbled something and left because I never seemed to bid enough. So my advice is: If you're a buyer, try bidding on a reserve auction, but don't spend a lot of time there. You'll soon learn whether a seller is a dreamer when it comes to how much money she thinks she's going to get. And if you're a seller: set realistic reserve prices that won't discourage sellers. Better yet—don't set a reserve and better observe how your auction progresses. If for some reason it's getting down to the wire and not enough has been bid in your opinion, then remove the item from eBay and be on your way.

➲ **Fixed price auctions.** You can experience these through eBay stores. To receive a designation as an eBay store, a seller needs to have a feedback score of 20 or higher and accept credit card or PayPal. eBay store items cost less to list, and can mean instant sales for the seller. If the price is right, then everyone's happy. As a buyer, browse eBay stores and see what's for sale—you know you'll get it faster, so if you can get it cheaper (or at least competitively priced) then go for it!

Question 14

When and How Does an Auction End?

An auction ends when the listing time has expired. That's the simple answer. It can end other ways too, and on many occasions, the ending is out of your control. An auction may even just end early. Let me explain.

➲ **The listing has expired with no bids:** If no one has placed a bid and the listing has expired, then the auction ends. Often a seller will relist, either "as is," or after making changes to the listing in order to make it more exciting to bidders.

➲ **The listing was removed by the seller:** A seller, for whatever reason, can decide to remove their item from eBay, losing any listing fees he has incurred. Sellers may do this because the item is no longer available (maybe they gave the tickets to a friend), there could have been a mistake in the listing or its description, or maybe the seller just was not happy with the bids he was receiving (or not receiving). He thought he was better off pulling the plug, rather than letting the item go for much less than he could afford.

⮑ **There was a winning bidder:** Someone won the auction because they outbid the competing bidders. Now that's more like it, that's what we're all here for.

I Won, So Now What?

Ahh, so *you're* the winning bidder! Congratulations! Before you do anything, let me suggest that you print out the listing page, just so you have it to review once the item comes. Also, keep the listing stored on your My eBay page, until such time that the entire deal is resolved.

Let me also recommend that you don't play armchair quarterback. Don't second guess yourself. Don't compare the amount you paid with other auctions that are still going on. No use crying over spilled bids.

You should hear from the seller within three days, but instead why don't you be a good sport and introduce yourself as the winner, in an e-mail. Give your name, address, and make sure you include the item number in all your correspondence. Reiterate what you believe to be the terms of the deal, such as, "I'm the winning bidder for item number ———, which was for $13.28. Shipping and handling is $4.95." Let the seller know how eager you are to receive the item, and confirm what payment methods they prefer and what shipping methods they use. (Will they offer insurance—for which you pay, of course. I recommend you insure your winnings).

Preferred payment methods are described in each item listing. Most accept PayPal, which is eBay's own online bill paying service. Still others accept money orders and personal checks (build in some time for the check to clear the seller's bank before your item ships). And you probably shouldn't send cash in the mail, for obvious reasons, but I confess to having sent some greenbacks to cover inexpensive auctions (but if the money got lost, that would have been my problem, not the seller's).

> *PayPal is eBay's payment system. By using PayPal the buyer and seller are protected against virtually any type of fraud.*

Anyway, back to PayPal. PayPal allows you to link your checking account and a credit card to your eBay account. You can instantly pay someone for an item by drawing out of one of your accounts, or charging it to Visa or MasterCard (you can even sign up for a PayPal credit card, but I personally thought that was a bit much!). PayPal charges you no service charges—those charges are borne by the sellers—and, like eBay, the service is perfectly safe and your account numbers are encrypted. And somewhere down the road, if you decide to sell on eBay (see Question 19) your auction sales will fund your own auction winnings, as buyers will be depositing money into your PayPal account. If you're serious about eBay, buying and/or selling, I suggest signing up for PayPal. Do so either through eBay's home page, or by logging on to *www.paypal.com.*

Once you're signed up to PayPal, you can pay for an item through your My eBay page (you'll see the item under Items I've Won), or you can go to the item listing page and click on *pay now.*

Not sure I have to say this, but...if you're using PayPal, make sure you have enough in your account to cover the expense. It gets embarrassing to not be able to pay for an item you won.

The Seller Says He Accepts Escrow—What Does That Mean?

Escrow is a service that allows you to send your payment to a seller to a third party, who then holds the payment until the funds clear. The money then gets remitted to the seller, who sends you your winning item. Escrow is good for when you're nervous and you're buying a big ticket item. Usually the buyer will pay the escrow fees, though sometimes they're borne by both parties who agree to do so. But to me, with PayPal protecting you, you'll get the same assurance from sending payment through PayPal.

Question 15

What Should I Do When I Receive My Order?

The UPS truck has a surprise for you today. The widget you bought from eBay is getting delivered to your door. Here are my suggestions on what to do when your winnings arrive:

- **Look at the package.** Make sure it doesn't have any obvious dents, smashes, or rips. Then carefully open it up. I've even read that you should have someone take pictures of you opening the package, just to protect yourself. That's paranoid, even for me, but I guess if you're sensing issues with this buyer, photos may help you defend youself, just in case.

- **Inspect the item.** Compare it to the listing—you did print out the listing right? Make sure it works, it's in the described condition, and that you're happy with what you received.

- **If you're happy with the item, then consider leaving positive feedback.** Refer to Question 8 for my feedback recommendations.

What if I Have a Problem With My Order?

First of all, don't panic. Take a deep breath, and don't get yourself in a tizzie. Try to trace where the problem first originated. For example:

⊃   **Check the listing:** Did you read the description correctly? Do you really know what you bought? If you bid in error, you obviously can't blame the seller for that.

⊃   **Check the packaging:** Could the item have been damaged in transit? If you purchased shipping insurance, you're covered (or at least you'll get your money back through the shipping service, but that may be no consolation when you consider your unique, one-of-a-kind item is now destroyed).

⊃   **Check the seller:** Could he have sent you the wrong thing? Is he willing to make good on the sale? If it was all just an honest mistake, maybe he'll easily give you your money back. I once sold someone an expensive comic book, shipped it with no problem, and the buyer was disappointed in its condition. I gave him his money back, including shipping. I got the comic back, and wound up selling it to someone else later. The original seller appreciated my customer service and gave me positive feedback (I returned the favor—and I also exchanged positive feedback with the new buyer). The key is communication—don't assume the seller was trying to rip you off. Work together towards a resolution.

If, however, you feel the seller owes you an explanation and/or a refund and he's being completely unreceptive or uncooperative, you may gain some assistance from eBay. The Buyer Protection program has a $25 deductible and you have to wait 30 days after the auction closes to get things rolling.

eBay also partners with *squaretrade.com* as a mediator to resolve disputes. Most problems can be straightened out through their online dispute resolution service. If that didn't help, you can get a human being involved and it will cost you about $20. Check out the SquareTrade site for all the details.

> *If something goes wrong with your transaction on eBay, there are a lot of different help options available to you. Buyer protection is an important part of the eBay system.*

PayPal also offers a measure of buyer protection (check out the site for all the details). Basically, you're insured for up to $200, with a $25 deductible. Nevertheless, I'll light a candle for you, that you will have no problems in your eBay buying. In the nearly 10 years I have been using eBay, I think I needed eBay's help twice, out of maybe 500 transactions. If you do your homework ahead of time, you'll work with the best sellers and buy the best items.

But do yourself a favor, don't get into a shouting match through feedback. Get the help you need, chalk it all up to experience, and move on to the next item.

Q*uestion* **16**

Are There Any Other Online Auction Sites?

Let me start this chapter off by saying that there are many Websites available on which one can bid on and buy things. You may even get the items at a tremendous savings. In my opinion, however, eBay is still the best. Nevertheless, I will share with you some of the others that are available, many of which are specialized for one type of item or another.

➲ **Half.com:** This is eBay's sister site, listing items for sale at a fixed price. The site is almost as diverse in its product offerings as eBay and in many regards, works the same way. You search for an item and when you find the closest matches, you will be brought to the item descriptions and price ranges from seller to seller. Sellers are also rated by feedback, and many sellers also sell on eBay. I would rate it right up there, just after eBay.

⮞ **Amazon:** The trend-setting online book retailer first entered the auction market in 1999 and are giving eBay a run for its money. They are the second-most active auction spot on the Web to you-know-who. With Amazon, you can begin buying and selling immediately without any special software to download. And although they have fewer items for sale than eBay, and eBay has better protection for buyer and seller, Amazon is at least worthy of a look.

⮞ **Froogle:** Owned by Google, obviously, this search engine scours the Web to see what like products are selling for online. You can then go right to that Website to buy, if you are interested. Or simply use Froogle to gather info, as you do your due diligence price comparisons.

⮞ **Yahoo:** Works like Froogle, searching the Web for vendors who are selling items you're looking for.

⮞ **Stubhub.com:** I'm a sports and concert fan and I thought this site would be for me, but I haven't been able to find many bargains here. Maybe you'll have better luck. It's easy to find information on the event or show you're interested in!

⮞ **Dealtime.com:** Similar to Froogle, in that it combines sales from a multitude of stores, but Froogle searches more extensively and gives you a wider variety of sales to choose from.

⮞ **Ubid.com:** Think eBay on a small scale, although I'm not quite sure how much protection you'll have here.

➲ **Priceline.com:** This is the largest of many online purveyors of travel deals. Check out other sites for travel, including *hotels.com* and *expedia.com*. Sites like this have their market, but I'm not the type who likes to take a flight at 3 a.m. with small children just to save $20 on my airfare.

> *There are plenty of other bidding and auction sites on the Internet for every interest such as Amazon, Froogle, Half.com, Stubhub.come and Dealtime.com. All of these sites are similar to eBay.*

Other online e-commerce sites include *overstock.com, bluelight.com* (Kmart's site), and *walmart.com*. I'm not sure you'll want to buy from them, but at least refer to the sites for price comparison purposes (see Question 7).

I present this chapter as a public service. I'm not promoting the services of these sites or any others (besides eBay of course!). Due to the nature of "here today, gone tomorrow" Websites, I'd hate to recommend that you send your hard earned money to an auction site or bidder, only to discover tomorrow that that URL doesn't exist anymore. Just be careful out there!

Question 17

Should I Buy From an eBay Seller Who Is Not Listing Items on eBay?

eBay frowns upon sales outside of eBay, for many reasons. Can you blame eBay for discouraging the buyer and seller from hooking up on their own? If people work on the side, then neither party needs eBay as a paid go-between and there go eBay's profits. The cockeyed optimist in me says, keep working exclusively through eBay, because then you have a level of protection afforded to both buyers and sellers. If you buy and sell on your own, who's to say a buyer won't run off with an item without paying or after sending a rubber check? What stops a seller from shipping you a piece of junk when you have no recourse? Remember, you can't post feedback on eBay unless a transaction took place, and you certainly can't ask SquareTrade to step in and solve your problems.

Let's put it this way: If you've dealt with a seller for some time, he's got great feedback, and you even have each other's personal e-mail addresses, odds are you will not have any problem buying and selling on your own. But I'm going to caution you: Don't communicate such deals through eBay—they monitor e-mails and they could run you out of eBay for violating their policies.

And don't tell anyone I told you to deal with anyone outside of eBay because I'll deny you heard it from me!

Question 18

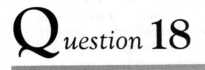

I Got an E-mail From eBay. What Should I Do?

You got an e-mail from eBay. It was all official looking, even including the eBay logo and links to click on. It basically said: we're doing a regular check of our records and we need you to verify your current account information. You are about to click where indicated and provide the information requested—after all, you want to behave like a good eBayer, don't you?

Not so fast, bucko. That e-mail did not come from eBay. It looked and sounded official, but it was sent by an unscrupulous hacker looking to attain sensitive information from you (including your credit card number, eBay password, or social security number). Commonly called phishing, such pirates are lurking online, attempting to sabotage your account and charge unauthorized purchases to it and, even worse, commit identity theft with your personal data. They even send you such messages through official looking PayPal e-mails—imagine what such geeks could do with all your financial information! If even one percent of eBay's users fall for these bogus e-mails, that's still millions of people that will keep these crooks in business.

If you get such an e-mail, know this: It's a scam. eBay will never ask for such information by e-mail. If eBay has something to tell you involving those subjects, they'll send you messages right to your account, which you can access through My eBay (see Question 6). Never give anyone your eBay or PayPal passwords, credit card number, or Social Security number.

eBay will never ask for any personal information such as credit card information, mailing addresses, names, or bank account information via e-mail. These e-mails you receive are created by scam artists trying to get personal information from you.

eBay is among the five companies most frequently targeted by phishers. Maybe it's because eBay relies on e-mailing so much in its normal course of business. If your user name too closely matches your e-mail address, scammers may pounce (see Question 3 for tips on coming up with a "safe" user name and password).

So if you get such a message, don't even click on any of the embedded links (or they may be able to get you later). Instead, forward the message to: *spoof@ebay.com.*

eBay strives to investigate such frauds and put an end to them. By forwarding these spoofs to eBay, you are helping out eBay and your fellow users.

Question 19

How Do I Sell on eBay?

By now, after reading this, I hope you're an ol' pro at eBay. I suspect you've bought many things, and met some interesting and helpful sellers to boot. By being a buyer, you learned a little bit about how to be a good seller from those you bought from. And odds are you might have bought "extra" of something and you wouldn't mind getting rid of it, or more specifically, selling it to someone who could use it.

So, are you ready to take the next step and cross over that line to the selling side of eBay? While it's easy to sell on eBay, to do it the right way takes work and attention. This chapter gives you some basic info for getting started, but there's so much more to learn.

The most important advice I would give prospective sellers is to observe other effective eBay sellers in action. What terms do they offer? How are their listings structured? Do they offer a guarantee? Do they charge actual shipping to their buyers, or a set shipping and handling charge? What have you learned about good customer service? Are you going to make eBay a legitimate money making business for you, or just a way to unload a few things in your basement? When you have positive experiences from buying from eBay sellers, print out the final listing page so you can refer to the seller's terms later. What do you think worked best, and what could you have done better, if you were a seller?

When you're ready to sell, it's time to get a listing together. Jot down on paper what you want to say. Take a photo of the item that you can include with the listing (eBay studies show that listings with photos sell better than those without. It seems people like to see what they're bidding on.) When you're ready, click on *sell* after logging on to your My eBay page. This will take you to the start of the sell area. Click *online auction*, and *sell your item* to move forward. eBay will then walk you through the process. You'll go from choosing the right category to sell in, proceed to writing a heading and item description, and then define the logistics of the sale (such as its duration, shipping charges, if you are shipping outside of the United States, and so on).

I'm Not so Sure About This. What Do I Do Now?

If you feel uncomfortable or unsure about anything involving selling your item on eBay, you can always stop working on the listing right where you are, even if you're halfway through the process. Listing an item for sale is always a work in process right up until you hit the last button: submit listing. You can back out at any time.

You know how I feel about feedback and its importance on eBay. With feedback, your reputation precedes you. If I were you, I would not list an item for sale until you are totally confident in what you're doing: that you've described and pictured the item properly, you're set up to accept payment (though PayPal or other choices), and you can pack the item properly and ship it in a timely manner. I would hate to have you get negative feedback from your buyer because you were a little green to eBay. Maybe it's time to study up on eBay selling and gain confidence.

> *Proceed slowly when you are selling an item for the first time. Always make sure you cover all the steps before officially listing something on eBay.*

You'll see in the next chapter that there are many books to give advice on buying on eBay. But I would bet that for every book dealing with eBay buying, there are probably five books on eBay selling, as more and more people are realizing the goldmine that's in their basements and garages if they were to sell these unwanted treasures on eBay. If you want to sell on eBay the right way, this chapter didn't do the subject justice. I would suggest you read and study some of these books dealing with starting an eBay business. To get you started, I suggest the sister volume to this book: *20 Questions to Ask Before Selling on eBay,* by Lissa McGrath.

Question 20

Where Can I Get More Information?

Congratulations, you're at the very end of the book. You've only just begun to eBay, as I've merely scratched the surface about buying on Ebay. There's only so much you can say in 100 or so pages. If you're even half the eBay junkie I am, you'll want to know more. As you might expect, there are a ton of places where you can get more information. Just about every publisher has seized the opportunity to publish books about the world's most popular online flea market. And there is tons of information online as well.

Books

There are hundreds of eBay books available. Among those are ones that include information helpful to eBay buyers (some seller information therein, too):

Collier, Marsha. *eBay Bargain Shopping For Dummies.* Hoboken, N.J.: Wiley Publishing Inc., 2003.

——————. *eBay Business All-in-One Desk Reference For Dummies.* Hoboken, N.J.: Wiley Publishing Inc., 2005.

——————. *eBay For Dummies, 4th edition.* Hoboken, N.J.: Wiley Publishing Inc., 2004.

——————. *eBay Timesaving Techniques For Dummies.* Hoboken, N.J.: Wiley Publishing Inc., 2004.

Ginsberg, Adam. *How to Buy, Sell & Profit on eBay.* New York: HarperCollins Lifestyle, 2005.

Holden, Greg. *CliffsNotes Buying and Selling on eBay.* Hoboken, N.J.: Wiley Publishing Inc., 2001.

——————. *eBay PowerUser's Bible.* Hoboken, N.J.: Wiley Publishing Inc., 2004.

McGrath, Lissa. *20 Questions to Ask Before Selling on eBay.* Franklin Lakes, N.J.: Career Press, 2006.

Miller, Michael. *Absolute Beginner's Guide to eBay, 3rd edition.* Indianapolis, Ind.: Que Publishing, 2005

——————. *Tricks of the eBay Masters.* Indianapolis, Ind.: Que Publishing, 2005.

Reno, Dawn and Bobby. *The Unofficial Guide to eBay and Online Auctions*. Hoboken, N.J.: Wiley Publishing Inc., 2000.

Schepp, Brad & Debra. *eBay Powerseller Secrets*. New York: McGraw-Hill, 2004.

Sinclair, Joseph T. *eBay Global the Smart Way*. New York: AMACOM, 2004.

————. *eBay Motors the Smart Way*. New York, N.Y.: AMACOM, 2004.

White, Terry et al. *Learn How to Buy and Sell on eBay for 5 Bucks*. New York: Pearson Education, 2004.

Wilkinson, Julia. *Ebay: Top 100 Simplified Tips & Tricks, 2nd edition*. Hoboken, N.J.: Wiley Publishing Inc., 2005.

[Here's a little tip: After you've bought one of more of the previously listed books and digested its information, why not sell that book on eBay and let someone else learn something?!]

Online

I was going to take this space to list some Websites that could provide information about eBay and buying online. But due to the fly-by-night nature of some sites, I was afraid the book would instantly become outdated. So I'll advise you to go to your favorite search engine and type in eBay and whatever related info you're curious about and see what matches come up.

The greatest source of eBay information online remains the eBay site itself. Take the time you need to surf the information on the eBay site. Try the chat boards in the Community section. And if you can't find information you're looking for, click on *live help* and find someone who can give you the answers.

Other Sources of Info

Seems like everyday there's an article about eBay in a newspaper or business publication, or a related news story on TV. Learn all you can about the eBay phenomenon. Attend a class about eBay. More and more people are looking to buy and sell on the site, and need more information. Check the bulletin of your local adult school, or course offerings from such national schools as The Learning Annex.